Let your light shine!

Matthew 5:14-16

Teresa Collins

Endorsements

" I found Teresa's book *'One Step Away – Finding Rest Through Loss'* both gripping and compelling. Suffering great loss in my own life it was refreshing to read an author who actually 'Gets it.' Teresa has faced incredible heartache, loss and grief throughout her life, yet she retains a simple, beautiful and childlike faith in the goodness of God. Despite every one of Teresa's losses, she never loses that upward glance, to where her hope resides. I was deeply moved in reading this book; you will also be."

_____ Tim Kelley

Senior Pastor of Grace Connection Church

Saint Petersburg, Florida

"I have felt your hurt and pain as I read your book. When I started reading, I couldn't put it down. I believe the love of Jesus made our paths cross. Our lives run parallel in so many ways. Looking forward to your next book. God Bless and Thank You for sharing how you got to where you are."

_____ Sharon Rucker

Retired Sheriff Deputy, Alabama

Obstetrical Nurse

"The words you've written have been guided by God and will surely help and encourage countless others."

_____ Clara Hinton

National Speaker, Certified Bereavement Facilitator,

Workshop Leader, Speaker, Blogger and Grief Coach

Author Silent Grief-Miscarriage-Child Loss – Finding your way

Child Loss: The Heartbreak and The Hope

www.SilentGriefsupport.com

"One Step Away – Finding Rest through Loss is an affirming message of hope and healing. Read and learn how to find the rest you've longed for."

_____ Frank Thomas

Coach, Consultant, Speaker

Author RISE: Even Death Can't Stop Me

www.thefrankthomasstory.com

www.facebook.com/irisebook

One Step Away

Finding Rest Through Loss

Teresa Collins

Publisher – Create Space Independent Publishing Platform
Edition 1st

ISBN-10:1515069354

ISBN-13: 978-1515069355

Printed in the United States of America

Dedication

To my Lord and Savior Jesus (Yeshua), you wrote the story of my life and knew each step would bring me closer to you. I give you all the praise and glory!

To my husband who has always encouraged and supported everything that I wanted to do or try. Thank You for your patience, love, and friendship…since 1989 and beyond.

To my adopted parents for giving me the love and opportunities, I would not have had otherwise.

To my sister as I know in those early years we were hand in hand trying to take care of each other and have grown into forever friends.

To my siblings even though we got a late start each one of you is special to my heart.

To my children and grandchildren, I loved each of you before I ever saw you.

In loving memory of my youngest son ~ you wanted me to be a part of your story, you were always a part of mine.

All of you have played a special role in who I am today.

Table of Contents

"It has been said; time heals all wounds. I do not agree.

The wounds remain. In time, the mind, protecting it's

Sanity covers them with scar tissue and the pain lessens.

But it is never gone"

~ Rose Kennedy

Foreword

Have you ever felt so alone in life that you've lost all hope? Have you experienced deep, profound losses such as the loss of marriage, the loss of a child, or the loss of life as you've once known it due to depression or abuse? Have you felt at times like you are lost in a world where you no longer belong? I've been through such deep sorrow and loss that there were times when I thought I couldn't face another day. I needed hope – the kind of hope that sustains a person through the toughest times in life. I needed the kind of hope that is given in the words penned for us in *One Step Away.*

One Step Away is a book that will grip your heart. You will identify with every word written in this book. It's a book that you will not want to put down, and you will read many times over. This book deals with the issues in life that very few people are courageous enough to share. Teresa Collins has given us more than just a glimpse into her life. She bares her soul to her readers. Teresa has felt the darkness of loss and abandonment. She knows what it's like to be in a situation after situation that dims all possibilities of hope. Yet, this author walks us gently down a path to a place of hope and rest.

If you're searching for hope, and you're feeling weary and need rest from the burdens of this life, then *One Step Away* is for you. Read it. Absorb the meaning behind the words. As you read *One Step Away,* you will find yourself breathing easier, gaining new insights into life's tragedies and pain, and you will be left feeling refreshed as you find your way to a place of peace and rest.

Clara Hinton

National Speaker, Certified Bereavement Facilitator, Workshop Leader, Author, Speaker, Blogger and Grief Coach.

Author of the books *Silent Grief* - Miscarriage – Child Loss: Finding your way *and*
 Child Loss: The Heartbreak and The Hope

www.SilentGriefsupport.com

You can also find Clara on Facebook at Silent Grief – Child Loss Support

PREFACE

What do you do when loss hits you out of the blue? How do you ease the pain? How do you go on? All these are food for thought. When I was faced with these questions, I had been hit by a devastating blow that knocked me completely off my feet. As I tried to get up, it seemed as if life was a bully that kept knocking me back down again and again… Everyone has a story. Some stories are filled with happiness with little challenges while others are filled with heartache and loss. This is one of those stories. The loss has touched my life leaving its many marks branded into my heart.

I often wonder what other people do when the pain of loss touches their lives. My experience has shown me that loss has an effect on you no matter how small it is, and it will demand your attention. Whether the loss is your own or happens to someone you love it will affect you deeply. The loss is painful, chaotic, sad and for me would take me to a place of helplessness.

Most people have experienced some kind of loss in their lives so what makes my story different? Every story is important, and every story has a journey that someone has walked through in a different way.

Walking down the memory lane of loss is difficult. The picture on the cover of this book tells it best. The sea of tears and the new sprout which represents the growth that came from every one of them. I had made up my mind after almost losing my own life to learning how to cope.

COPE - to face and deal with responsibilities, problems, or difficulties, successfully or in a calm or adequate manner.

Whether you witness the addiction of a family member or struggle yourself. Have you been abused by words or actions? Every parent's nightmare is to have their child stolen. Afraid of being abandoned? Whether you or someone you know has experienced the devastating impact of abortion. Have you lost a house, job or pet? All of these have one thing in common; they are all loss! It reaches into your heart and squeezes the life out of you.

Verbally telling my story was hard enough but writing it was almost torture.

My writing journey has been a difficult one as these words were written in the midst of many tears. The losses left an imprint on my memory and a hole in my heart. How do I calm the pain? How do I fill the hole that loss has so painfully left? These are the questions I needed to answer….so my journey began. There were days I didn't know if I would be able to finish this book, in the midst of my misery I would get stuck. I put the pen down, took a break, took a deep breath and found the strength to continue. I accomplished my goal, the written story of my journey through loss.

Follow me on my journey and experiences as I navigate through the difficult process of personal change to show you how I am making it through my many losses. I hope by giving you a glimpse into my life that you are able to glean some hope, encouragement and rest as you face loss in your own life.

MY STORY MY LIFE
INTRODUCTION

What is the meaning of loss? Many times we encounter life experience that sticks to our memories forever. Many of these instances we encounter losses that come in different forms. The loss is simply a state of having something taken away from you or a state of being deprived of something. Loss can be in a form of an abduction, abuse, adoption, abortion, addiction (loss of self-control), death, depression (loss of happiness), neglect, divorce or abandonment. No single person is excluded when it comes to life losses. At least at one point in your life, you must have lost somebody close to you or felt it through the experiences of others. No one can compare loss. The greatest loss is the one that you are experiencing.

Life losses often result in a helpless feeling, hopelessness, and discouragement. There are so many emotions when you experience loss. You may feel shock or disbelief, anger, guilt, sadness, anxiety, depression. Physical symptoms such as sleeping, breathing, eating issues, lack of energy, body weakness and restlessness follows. It is because of these issues that some people opt to drugs or suicide at extreme levels. Grieving after a loss may seem disturbing but a necessity in the healing process and the amount of time it takes is different for everyone. The feeling one has after encountering a loss can best be described as an agonizing cry from the heart which seems not to have any answers. It is said that grief has five stages, but I think there are more. At times, it felt like my system was being bombarded with so many emotions at once I wasn't sure which stage I was in. I felt hysterical and then other times I felt I couldn't cry at all. I want to share my story which may be very emotional to some readers, but it is important that I speak out. When I was going through various challenges, I didn't have anyone to call. I felt it was important to include resources so if you find yourself in any of these situations you have contact information to get help. Walk with me as I unfold my life experiences. If you are reminded of a familiar place on your own path, grab a pen and write it down. There is healing that can come from writing through the pain.

CHAPTER ONE
ADOPTION

Adoption – *taking and accepting something as one's own though originally not yours.*

I was born in the summer of 1953 to a teen mother in South Florida. I was never told the time or my size. Two years later, my sister was also born in the same location, after which it took a little while before we moved to Northeast Ohio. Closets were our homes; I remember how the bottom door cracks were the only source of light in our dark life. At this young age, alone with soggy diapers, I could already feel the loss of time and attention from my mother.

At four, my maternal grandfather along with his wife came to pick me up. I sat on my stepgrandmother's lap the entire 1000-mile road trip to the south chattering non-stop. My sister, on the other hand, would just go across town to live with my maternal grandmother. Despite the fact that I had a new family, I felt the pain of losing my mother, sister and the environment setting that I was used to. It is surprising how my step-grandmother would narrate to me telling me how I was afraid staying in the dark and I wouldn't dare take off my shoes. What shocked me most was when she told me that I had never at a point in time cried or asked for my father or mother. Hugs and close attention were all I needed at the age of four.

Life felt better with the feel of attention and love around me; I was getting spoiled. We went to the court and a judge in a black robe told me that I had a new mother and father. I remember holding their hands as we walked out of that courtroom as one united family. I was then raised as the only child. I was sensitive and shy; I had a good imagination, so boredom was never an issue. I had sandy blonde hair with skin browned from the sun, outside and barefoot was my favorite place to be as the weather was warm all year. I could swim and chase grasshoppers in the backyard.

I saw my biological father a few times but never had a chance to form a deeper parental relationship with him. When I was in grade school, he moved back to the Indian Reservation in Canada. It was so unfortunate that he passed away after a few years and was buried there. I never knew his relatives, but I did receive a letter from one of his sisters. She listed the names of her brothers, sisters and my grandparents. This letter brought tears to my eyes and joy to my heart as it was special to know their names. She indicated that it was a large family. She promised photos but since I have lost track of her and unable to connect with any other family members I was unable to receive them.

It was not until I was in middle school that I would feel the pain of being adopted. It was unbearable and hard to accept. It came out of the mouth of a bully that my own mother didn't want me; other kids would join in the fun as my tears would show my weakness. They cascaded down my face; I was already too weak to accept what life had prepared for me. I had to live with the confusion of life that was full of sadness, separation, and rejection amidst the new love and comfort of my new life. I couldn't understand the reason why my mom threw me away, what was wrong with me that seemed to mark me "the unwanted." I later learned that I had four siblings who had a close bond since they were raised close to each other. I never stopped thinking about what my life would be like if we were all raised together.

I didn't have the opportunity to be raised in a Christian home; the only chance that came my way was to visit different churches and summer vacation bible school with my friends. Since my mother didn't drive, we would walk to a church a few blocks away on occasion. These memories have never left my mind. I even remember one incident when I woke up in the middle of the night, and it was dark, the living room light had burnt out. I was so afraid of the dark that I wanted to run to my parent's room. I thought something could grab me by my feet. I remembered the love of Jesus upon my life and quickly threw the cover back and ran fast.

I also remember vividly, in 1968 when I was 15, I went to the movies and watched a movie entitled "For Pete's Sake." The movie was so touching that I couldn't hold back my tears. After the movie, there was an alter call to which I responded and decided to give my life to Jesus. This marked a significant event in my life. A new beginning, a faith beginning that marked a new foundation.

The 5 Stages of Adoption Adult Development

Adoption remains an important aspect of identity throughout adulthood, and one study described the development of adult adoptive identity as having five stages.

- ❖ **No awareness/denying Awareness** – The adopted person does not overtly acknowledge adoption issues.

- ❖ **Emerging Awareness** – The adopted person views adoption as a positive influence and recognizes some issues, but he or she is not ready to explore these issues.

- ❖ **Drowning Awareness** – The adopted person has feelings of loss, anger and sadness about the adoption.

❖ **Re-emerging from Awareness** – The adopted person recognizes the issues related to the adoption but also sees the positive aspects and is working toward acceptance.

❖ **Finding Peace** – The adopted person has worked through his or her issues with the adoption and is moving towards peace and acceptance.

(Penny, Boarders & Portnoy, 2007) Child Welfare Information.

As a preteen, I still struggled with being adopted. I didn't understand why my mother had given both my sister and I up, and why she would separate us from each other. I accepted my adopted mother though we didn't share even a drop of blood. She was never able to have any children of her own, so I was her little girl. I loved her and my grandfather very deeply.

Soon, my teen years were upon me, and it would bring some difficult challenges.

CHAPTER TWO
ABUSE

Abuse – *treated with cruelty or violence regularly and repeatedly, wrongful practices or improper treatment by a person on another.*

I started going for dance lessons at four. Tap was my favorite and what I was good at. I was introduced as the girl with the educated feet. The announcer would say that my feet were like those of Eleanor Powell, and I looked like Nancy Sinatra. I wasn't very familiar with them, but I

considered myself to be pretty and a good dancer.

My father liked charity shows and would organize the event for the area nursing homes. He would bring together different actors and talented individuals. The variety show would last for an hour. A boy and his sister would do tricks on a unicycle with the brother balancing his sister on his shoulders.

After a couple of dating years, this boy and I got married. I was 17 and had a son, sixteen months later I would have my second son. It is at this point that my life took a sharp turn again. I endured abuse and lost trust. It was the secrets of the dark.

The room is dark, and pain is starting to set in. I used the wall to support myself on my wobbly legs as I was shaking. I could hardly see.

I managed to make my way to the bathroom mirror. I was gasping as I caught a glimpse of myself. The reflections frightened me as though they weren't mine. I dabbed the blood around the corners of my mouth and nose. Tears were trying to squeeze through my swollen eye tissue that was turning blue.

I sat and rested my body as I watched his rage-filled face. It kept sending more memories into my mind.

Suddenly, I heard him open the door and made his way in. I heard his footsteps, I froze, afraid to breathe.

"Did I really do that to you?" I heard the concern in his voice.

I couldn't say anything; I was numb, afraid to speak. I just sat there hurting so much with tears rolling down my cheeks.

Maybe this is what I deserved, I thought to myself.

"I'm sorry." He said as he grabbed my hand, I was startled by his touch.

I removed the ice from my face and tried to open my eyes. I heard him gasp. I felt his head in my lap as he collapsed in tears.

"I can't believe I did this to you again." He cried.

"It was just an accident; you didn't mean it." My voice trembled as I tried to speak.

I couldn't move; I just sat there embarrassed and weak.

I reluctantly put my hand on his head to comfort him.

"I am sorry I let you down," I whispered.

"I'm sorry; I will never do this to you again." He said through his sobs.

I was torn between relief and fear; I wanted to believe him. My head was spinning; the love, the anger, the promises, the pain. The words I had heard so many times before, the love I desperately needed from him would be at the end of each attack. I would be in seclusion for weeks until the bruises would fade, the swelling and cuts would heal. I felt like a prisoner in my own home. Each time I wanted to leave, each time I stayed. I believed him this time; I believed he would really change.

The Four Psychological Stages of the battered women syndrome:

Denial – I thought it would always get better, I believed the promises of 'I'll never do it again.'

Guilty – I blamed myself for his actions.

Enlightenment – I don't deserve to be treated like this, but I will give it another chance.

Responsibility – I realize that it would happen again because it was always the same promises.

(The 2015 Stop Violence Against Women)

One out of every four women, is a victim of domestic violence. More than 60% of these cases happen at home. Women between the ages of 18-34 are at the greatest risk of being victims of domestic violence. More than 4 million women experience physical assault and rape by their partners. It is shocking that in every 2 out of 3 female homicide cases, a woman is killed by either a family member or intimate partner. This is the reason as to why more than three million children witness domestic violence every year.

You are not alone.

You are not to blame.

You do not deserve to be treated this way.

You have rights.

You can get help!

Safe Horizon 2015 1-800-621-HOPE (4673)

Sadly, I didn't make the call and experienced this abuse over and over again. It was hard for me to trust. The worst part of it was that abuse came from people I put my trust in, people I loved. I encountered all sorts of abuses ranging from emotional, physical and verbal. Abuse comes in many forms, remember Love equals respect. If you feel like you are in an abusive situation, you are not alone. I was scared and always thought the relationship would change, but it didn't, and the abuse continued. I ended up feeling like a prisoner to my abuser. Afraid that if I stood up to him, the abuse would get more violent. The silence only made me a victim. If you are in an abusive relationship, take a stand for yourself! Make the call! You are worth it!

CHAPTER THREE
ABDUCTION

Abduction – *to seize, hold, carry off a person by force, to steal a child.*

When my second son was a month old, my husband was involved in an automobile accident in which he suffered a broken neck. His spinal cord was severed leaving him paralyzed from the neck down. I was now a single parent. I lost my husband, and the boys lost their dad. He spent the next year in a rehabilitation center a few hundred miles away. It was hard for the boys and I to visit as I didn't drive and it wasn't always convenient for others to take us. His parents lived a state away, they never came to visit or contacted us.

Months later, I was outside watching the children play amazed at how much they had grown over the last few months. The warm breeze felt so good after the long winter it would dance through their curls as their white hair sparkled in the bright sunshine. I was amused by the baby trying to copy everything his big brother was doing. To my surprise the grandparents showed up unexpectedly with my husband in the car. I was excited to see him, but I soon learned that they were on a different mission. They said they stopped by to take the children to see their aunt about an hour away. I thought it was nice of them to think of the boys like that. The older boy was three, and the younger one was 18 months. The boys glanced at me for a reassuring look as they didn't know their grandparents. Grandma took the older boy; he was unsure but went with her. Grandad started poking fun at him in the car. The baby was quiet, but I could see a hint of a smile as he watched his brother's fun.

"I will see you guys in a little bit," I said as I gave them each a kiss. " Have fun!"

"We will bring them back after a few hours," Grandad said as he got some giggles from the boys.

When they left, I felt a little lost as the boys were such a big part of my life. They were my life! I was eager to see them return.

Three hours, four hours, five hours' time was ticking with no glimpse of their appearance until it got dark. At this point, I was getting worried. I paced wondering about all the possibilities, could they have been in an accident, where they broke down along the side of the road or had time just slipped away as they visited. Crazy thoughts continued to fill my mind. I finally made up my mind and decided to give them a call. I knew for sure no one would answer.

"Hello?" Grandma answered.

I quickly hung up the call and sat there confused on what to do next. Why did they decide to take them to their place?

I have to go and get them. My mind was racing as I began to walk in circles. Why didn't they call me? Did they take my boys? Questions kept running through my head. They never called, and I was afraid to call them again. I had to think; I had to find someone to help me....

I found a friend that would drive me to get my boys. I knew it was going to be a long drive that would take us into the morning hours. As we made our way through the early morning fog, I saw a building with a sign that said 'Justice of the Peace.'

I rushed in and out of breath; I stood at the counter.

"Please, I need your help!"

"Ma'am slow down, what is the problem?" The officer asked curiously.

" My in-laws came yesterday morning and asked if they could take the boys to see an Aunt who lived an hour away and never came back then I called, and they answered the phone at their home." I was running out of breath.

"I think they have kidnapped my boys," I said with sadness.

"Are you married to their father?" asked the officer.

"Yes, he is in a rehab right now. He broke his neck in an accident and is paralyzed from the neck down." I explained.

"Ma'am He has just as much right to the children as you do."

"It wasn't him it was his parents," I said

"Ma'am it's a civil matter, we can't get involved." He said firmly.

"I have to get my kids!" I stated.

" You can take them back just the same." He said

I was scared. They wouldn't help me but confident as I remembered that he said they were my kids too. So I continued on my way.

It had been a while since I had been on that long country road but it was still familiar. I could feel the butterflies as I saw the house. I pulled in the drive and sat for a moment to gather my courage. My friend wanted to stay in the car and wait.

I knocked on the door. Grandma opened it.

"Come in." she said.

"Mommy Mommy!" My son screamed with delight as he tackled me with hugs. I grabbed him up giving him kisses and hugs as I held him tight.

"Where's the baby?" I asked.

"He's in the back bedroom taking a nap," Grandma said.

I put my son down, took his hand and walked back to get the baby. I peeked in the bedroom, and when our eyes met, he laughed with excitement. I picked him up and cradled him in my arms.

I had the baby on my hip and my son by the hand. When I stepped into the hall, Grandad was standing there with grandma behind them.

"Where do you think you are going?" Grandad asked.

"I'm leaving with my kids!" I said as I pulled them close.

Grandad pried my son's hand from mine, and Grandma took him to another room.

"Mommy mommy!" He cried with his arms stretch out for me to help him.

I held tightly to the baby with both arms.

"Give me the boy," Grandad said sternly.

"No! Why are you doing this?" I yelled as I tried to push by him, the baby began to cry.

Grandad pushed the baby and me against the wall and started pulling the baby up by his arms, I held on tight around his waist.

"Please! Don't take my babies!" I begged. I felt a blow on my head, I was stunned but continued to hold on to my baby. I could still hear my son screaming in the other room.

I felt another blow to my head; I kicked and fought to no avail. My baby was snatched from my arms with another crushing blow to my stomach from Grandad. Grandma took the baby from Grandad; he was kicking and screaming as I fell to the floor. I had lost.

I was hurt, humiliated and defeated. I could hear my babies crying desperately for me. I begged again through my sobs, "Please don't take my babies!"

"It's time for you to leave now," Grandad said as he forced me to stand, pushing and half carrying me out of the house. I sat in the car numb, confused and angry about what had just happened.

I could hardly see through my tears as I made my way back to the Justice of the Peace office.

"Ma'am what happened?" The officer asked.

"Grandad assaulted me and took my babies right out of my arms, and I'd like to file an assault charge," I said firmly.

When the case was taken to court, the grandparents lied, saying they had a house full of company on that day. My friend couldn't testify as he didn't witness anything inside the house. Several people lied boldly under oath and said that no one had touched me that day. It was my word against theirs; that's what the lawyer said.

I was issued with divorce papers from my paralyzed husband at this hearing; the grandparents were awarded temporary custody because they had possession of the children at the time. I lost again.

My dad hired an attorney to fight on my behalf, but the attorney seemed to be full of excuses of delayed court dates. I was issued with divorce papers at the hearing of the assault. I didn't contest because I felt he didn't love me anymore. Time was moving on, and one excuse was that I was a single mother, and the court wouldn't look favorably on that. After a few months, I married again. He was in the military with orders to Korea. This round the excuse was that we had to wait until he got back from overseas. That was a 13-month tour. Then the excuses continued; that the Courts were congested, snow storms…. on and on and on. I told my dad that something was wrong, and he said lawyers were busy people. I was always prepared and ready for the return of my boys. I was allowed to visit, so I got to see them from time to time. Time passed and seasons changed with no progress. I felt like every day, every birthday; every holiday was another loss.

I lost so much during this time; it knocked me completely off my feet. I lost my children, but I didn't do anything wrong to deserve it so I couldn't understand how that was allowed to happen. I didn't understand how one person could hurt another person so badly, but I remembered seeing that same rage-filled face before, it was the face of abuse from my husband, Grandad's son. I thought about how abuse runs in families, and now my sweet little boys were in their care. Their screams will never fade from my memory.

"Why do family members take children? Is it love? Usually not, the typical motivation for family abduction is power, control, and revenge. Family abduction is a form of family violence.

The abduction of a young child will have a significant influence on the kind of person he or she becomes. Time does not heal the wounds when the left-behind family remains in a state of limbo. Time, unfortunately, provides additional triggers, and pain: the child's birthday, the anniversary of the child's abduction and the holidays. Families of abducted children experience serious emotional distress. Most families live for the moment when they will be united with their children." *Used by permission Georgia K. Hilgeman-MA Retired Executive Director and Founder, Vanished Children's Alliance (see Resources for information).*

Have you ever been afraid that your child will be kidnapped by a stranger? Did you know that it's much more common for a child to be taken away by a parent or another family member? Some people think that you can't steal something that's already yours, but when it comes to a child, that's not true. Children are not like a piece of property; it hurts them when they are forcefully secluded and kept from other people they care about.

It's a crime for a parent, relative, or any other person to take away, hide, or keep a child from the other parent or a person who has rights to the child. Nearly 262,100 children are abducted every year 58,200 non-family and 203,900 family abductions. I didn't have this information when this happened to me so I'd like to share it with you just in case it would happen to you or someone you know. If you have any questions about child-stealing, call your local District Attorney's Office. **The National Center for Missing and Exploited Children (NCMEC) 1-800-843-5678 or Find the Children 1-888-447-6721**

(See Resources for information)

I found all of these statistics to be true from my experience. This information helped me to know that what the grandparents did, in this case, was wrong and in some small way gave me a feeling of justice. I wish I would have had this information when my boys were abducted. If you or anyone you know is experiencing this, please share this information with them! There are no words to describe losing a child whether you know where they are or not...it's an anguishing, heartbreaking traumatic loss.

CHAPTER FOUR
ABORTION

Abortion - *deliberate termination of a human pregnancy with destruction of the embryo or fetus.*

The year was 1974, right after the decision of Roe V. Wade (that abortions are permissible for any reason a woman chooses until the point at which the fetus becomes viable, that is potentially able to live outside the mother's womb without artificial aid. The court also held that abortion after viability must be available when needed to protect the woman's health. At the time Roe was decided; most states severely restricted or banned the practice of abortion.)

I was in a vulnerable place in my life as I had a lot of pain I couldn't control. I had gone through a traumatic event with the abduction of my children then was assaulted with my babies being ripped right out of my arms. Then I felt like the legal system further abused me with the attorney telling me it was unfavorable for me to go to court for my boys without a husband. I was looking for something, anything to help. I met a guy who offered sensitivity, understanding and a soft place to land. One thing led to another, and a few months later I realized I was pregnant with his child. I love children so when I found out I was happy and eager to share the news with him. When I told him, I was pregnant everything changed. He was cold and uncaring at the point of being harsh as he pushed me away. He didn't want anything to do with me. I was living in the northern states, so I made arrangements to go back down south to stay with my parents.

When I got home, my dad told me I couldn't live with this mistake for the rest of my life. He told me I needed to get an abortion, but I knew he wouldn't take me to a back alley butcher shop that is where I thought abortions were done. I didn't fully understand the decision of Roe V. Wade at that time until my dad made the appointment at an abortion clinic.

Daddy, please don't make me go. The words played over and over in my head.

Numb and confused I walked into the clinic.

"Can I help you?" the lady at the window asked.

"I would like to talk to someone please," I whispered.

"Have a seat someone will be with you in a few minutes." She said.

I hung my head as I looked around for a seat I was relieved to see that no one else was there.

The door opened, I followed the lady to a room with a desk and two chairs. She closed the door.

"I am 11 and half weeks pregnant," I said quietly.

"How does that make you feel?" she asked.

"I love children, but when the guy found out, he stopped talking to me." I continued.

"I went home to stay with my parents, and my dad is unhappy," I said sadly.

"He wants me to get rid of it." I choked on the words.

"Well honey, at this stage it's just a blob of tissue, it's not really a baby yet." She said.

"Are you sure?" I asked.

"I'm very sure!' she replied.

She assured me that the whole process would be quick and painless.

The date was set.

I wanted to keep my baby, but I never wanted to disappoint my dad. He spoke to me with such a firm tone in his voice which I wasn't used to hearing and I know he was trying to protect me. I felt like I had to go through with it.

The day came.

"Daddy, please don't make me go!" I begged.

"You can't live with this for the rest of your life." He argued.

"He told me that he loved me, daddy," I replied softly.

I got in the backseat with my face buried in the door.

We walked into the clinic. I felt desperate. I wanted to turn and run back out the door.

I can't disappoint my dad, I thought.

I was greeted by the same lady I spoke with when I made the appointment. I followed her to a room with an exam table; the stirrups were up and ready. She told me to undress from the waist down, position myself on the table with my heels in the stirrups and place the paper drape over my knees.

"Someone will be in shortly." She said as she left and pulled the door closed behind her.

Well, this is it, I thought with a big sigh. I glanced around the room there was a tray of instruments and a big bottle with a hose.

She said it would be quick and painless, I remembered.

The door opened, two people appeared dressed in green from head to toe. I was alarmed to see them all covered up like that. They didn't speak to me until I heard a male voice tell me to slide my bottom down to the end of the table.

I took a deep breath with tears filling my eyes.

The procedure began.

Beads of sweat formed on my forehead as I fought back the urge to cry out from the pain. The machine connected to the bottle was loud, and the bottle was filling up with what looked like blood. I could hear the male voice talking in some sort of code and a female voice answer.

It was quick but far from painless.

I sat in the recovery area sipping orange juice. I thought about all the blood and blobs of tissue being sucked into that big bottle.

It's done. I lost my baby.

I was numb, empty, angry and ashamed. I was silent all the way home and for days after that.

It was about five years later I was sitting in church, and the sermon was about abortion. I learned a devastating truth.

Psalm 139:13-16 you made all the delicate, inner parts of my body and knitted me together in my mother's womb. Thank you for making me so wonderfully complex! Your workmanship is marvelous—how well I know it. You watched me as I was being formed in utter seclusion, as I was woven together in the dark of the womb. You saw me before I was born. Every day of my life was recorded in your book. Every moment was laid out before a single day had passed.

My baby had a heartbeat at about 6 weeks, arms and legs were moving at 8 weeks and 11 and a half weeks my baby's critical systems were fully formed, the baby would move if you poked it which means the baby could feel. My baby was over an inch long and weighed 0.30 ounces. I learned that the procedure I had done was the suction method which rips the baby limb by limb then they crush the head and pull it out.

There was no ultrasound available to see my baby's heartbeat or see him sucking his thumb as he moved around in his sanctuary.

It wasn't a blob of tissue! I wanted to scream.

I killed my baby! I could hardly breathe.

They lied! I was in anguish.

I put my face in my hands as my tears accompanied my uncontrolled sobbing. How could I have done such a thing? I thought.

I felt physically sick.

How could God let me live after I had committed such a merciless act? I wondered.

Psalm 103:10; He does not punish us for all our sins; he does not deal harshly with us, as we deserve.

58,586,256

Abortion Statistics since Roe V. Wade

National Right to life Educational Foundation

Are you pregnant and confused Call ProLife America Hotline 1-800-712-4357 Counselors24/7?

(See Resources for information)

Please let your baby live!

As the days turned into weeks, weeks turned into months; months turned into years I was feeling the loss of my boys and my unborn baby more and more. I was sinking in the depths of despair, and depression. Depression is the loss of happiness. I knew I was going to need some help, so I went to see a psychiatrist. He gave me several medications which only seemed to make me not care about what had happened or life itself. It was at this time I tried to end my life. I knew how it felt to have a broken heart, my whole body hurt. I just wanted it to stop! The only way I knew this could happen was to be with Jesus. He promises there would be no more pain and no more tears.

I had a neighbor, a middle school aged girl, who lived across the street that always left for school about the same time I was leaving for work we would always talk a little bit as our paths crossed. Since she didn't see me out that morning, she came to check on me. She peeked through the screen door saw me lying on the sofa put two and two together and got help. She was my little angel that day.

My stomach was pumped, and I found myself in a locked unit in the hospital. A few days later I was finally awake and glad I was still alive. I stared out the window wondering how all the people out there were able to handle their losses; I was sure they had at least one. I asked the doctor to stop giving me the lithium shots I didn't want to feel numb all the time. I wanted to feel, and I wanted to learn how to cope. When I was in the hospital, the doctor told me my dad had passed away. It felt like the end of the world right then, and I was glad I was in a place where I had someone to talk to. I was on a quest to find freedom from using drugs or anything else to cover my pain. I had experienced pain on the inside that was so intense to an extent that it hurt all the way to the outside. I was affected mentally, emotionally and physically. I was on a journey to find the strength to endure the pain and learn how to rest in the midst of the pain.

Have you ever hurt this bad?

Every 78 seconds a teen attempts suicide – every 90 seconds they succeed.

National Center for Health Statistics

I was able to attend my dad's funeral. He was the only dad I ever knew and a vital part of my life. I didn't have much of an extended family, and my siblings were still far away. I wasn't sure I would ever make it without him. At this point, I had multiple losses overlapping each other.

I have felt the emptiness and loss of my unborn baby until this day. It took time, a long time to work through the anger with my dad. I finally learned how to forgive him and myself. I pray for those who perform abortions, those who get them and the babies who lose their lives. Let the babies live!

In my twenties, I had suffered abuse, was given up for adoption, abused again, lost my husband to an accident and then to a divorce, lost my children by a violent abduction, lost my unborn baby, lost my dad and almost lost my mind and my life. If you need help call the **National Suicide Prevention Lifeline 1-800-273-TALK (8255) anytime 24/7Deaf or Hard of Hearing TTY 1-800-799-4889 Immediate Medical Crisis Call 911(see Resources for information)**

My journey to find rest continued…

CHAPTER FIVE
ABANDON

Abandon – *to forsake completely, desert, leave behind, to give up something begun before completion, discontinue, and withdraw from.*

We do encounter losses in our lives after relationships come to an end.

My oldest son had a daughter, but his relationship came to an end with her mother, so they parted ways. He was in another relationship in which he had a son but in the meantime he had reconciled with his daughter's mother. When my grandson was born, my son told me I wasn't allowed to have his daughter in my life if I had a relationship with my new grandson. You can imagine the torment of the situation I found myself in. I would either lose both of them or one of them. I was faced with a dilemma but had to make a decision. I told my son it wasn't fair, but he wouldn't listen or reason with me. I felt like my son was in the wrong by putting me in such a position to have to choose between my grandchildren. It drove a wedge between us. Sadly, I wouldn't see or hear from my son or granddaughter for years after that. To me, these were two more losses.

Four years later I got a call from a friend of my grandson's mother telling me to go and get him. When I arrived, I found my grandson with a note written by his mother pinned on his shirt. The message on the note indicated that his mother had abandoned him, and my husband and I were to take care of him. This reminded me of how my mother had abandoned me when I was only four; now the same was happening to my grandson. He had no belongings, so I just got hold of him, and we went home. My son, his dad and I were not speaking and were not on good terms at this moment, but I felt it was right that he knew what was happening with his son. This was a boy he had never even wanted to have a relationship with, but I felt it was important for him to come and visit him. To my surprise, he came to visit. The visit went well, and his son was very comfortable around him and his wife. After that visit with his son ended, he wanted to visit again and again. Healing was setting in.

A little while after that my son decided that he wanted to raise him. I felt this wasn't a bad idea as his son was excited about it too. Our relationship was healing, and my grandson had his dad.

When my grandson's mom found out that his dad had him, she got a Judge to write a court order so she could get him back. The police took my grandson away from my son and returned him back to the same mother who had abandoned him at a friend's house by pinning a note to his shirt. My son hired an attorney, but he found himself in the same position that I was in many years earlier when I was trying to fight for him and didn't have the money to do so. I would console him in his grief which was a painful reminder of my own case. We shared the loss of our sons in common.

My daughter was the typical girl next door. She was beautiful, funny, cared about people and a little naive. She had been influenced by a lifestyle that would systematically tear her and her life apart. Money was easy coupled with an abundance of attention that pulled her in. I saw her sink further and further into the depths of darkness. I watched as it would strip her away little by little – her dignity, health personality, innocence, and spirit.

I was so frustrated and concerned about her safety. She was consumed by her addictions and the passion of an exotic dancer. It was such a terrible time as I felt I was losing her, there seemed to be so much distance between us. This went on for 15 years. She had two daughters who she loved dearly, but they were abandoned in her world of work and confusion. Her busy lifestyle wouldn't allow her to give the girls the attention they deserved. It got to the point that the girls needed a change. Her teen daughter was placed with me, and her younger sister went with her dad. Not only did I experience the loss of my daughter but also watched my daughter lose her children. Her resentment towards me made our differences more intense. This was a very painful time. This was a web of losses that hurt all of us.

A few years later, I got in a committed 5-year relationship. He also abandoned me, walked out on me and never came back. I watched and waited for over a year with no return of him. I suffered a lot emotionally after this relationship ended. I lived with shame for quite some time and stopped trusting people. Would I be accepted or rejected? I questioned my values. I was afraid of getting into another relationship or expressing my feelings. This again reminded me of the abandonment that happened when I was only four years old. It had happened again; someone supposed to love me had walked out on me with no explanation. The feeling of worthlessness, not being good enough and wondering why I was unlovable continued to weigh on me.

Stay with me as we go a little deeper...

CHAPTER SIX
CHAINS

C **hains** - *a connected flexible series of links, typically metal used to hold objects together, bonds, fetters or shackles, captivity, oppression or bondage.*

I married my second husband with whom I had a beautiful daughter. After 6 years I delivered a special-needs handicapped son. My son was delivered at 32 weeks through the emergency C- section. I developed a condition called toxemia with preeclampsia during my pregnancy; my baby boy weighed 3 pounds 4 ounces. We were both clinging to life by a life-support machine. He had under-developed lungs while I suffered from heart failure during his delivery. I was able to see him, a week later, for the first time in the Neonatal Intensive Care Unit. It was overwhelming, the flashing lights, beeping monitors, the tangle of tubes and an incubator with my tiny baby boy inside as he was surrounded by various pieces of equipment. He would spend almost a year in the hospital's NICU (Neonatal Intensive Care Unit) with me by his side as much as I could be. His sister was just starting kindergarten and needed me too. This was a very draining time for me, one minute he was doing fine and then the next minute I would get a bad report; it was an emotional roller coaster ride. I watched everything that was done and knew his treatments, his medication doses, and feeding schedule. At one point I assured the doctors, I was able to manage his care at home. Almost a year later, he was able to come home weighing twelve pounds, he was unable to sit up, needed to be on oxygen, and required around-the-clock treatments which I would give him. He suffered from oxygen deprivation and also had a chronic lung disease that was caused by over-inflation of his lungs to save his life. Many doctors and Health Care professionals were a part of this life from the very beginning; neurologist, psychiatrists, psychologist, physical therapists, and special classes in school. At the age of two, his dad and I divorced. I didn't want to walk out but without the help of counseling, things were getting out of control. I didn't have hope. I had already been abused and knew I had to make a final decision to stop the reoccurrence. When my son was eight, I married the wonderful man with whom I live with today; we have been together for 26 years. He loved my son, and my son called him dad.

When he started school, they insisted that he be put on Ritalin. He continued on this until the end of the seventh grade. I discontinued the medication as I was tired of seeing his zombie-like behavior. I home schooled him for the eighth and ninth grades. He wanted to try school again for the 10th grade. They wanted to mainstream him, but he wasn't able to manage the work, he was getting frustrated and falling behind. I felt like he was falling through the cracks of the school system. By the time I got the 504 handicap plan in place, he had given up and quit. He was realizing his disability for the first time through harsh words and finger pointing from his peers. As much as I watched over his health, I was unable to protect him from those who wanted to hurt and make fun of him.

Low self-esteem, depression, anxiety, suicidal thoughts would require extra care both mentally and physically. At one of his counseling sessions, I learned that he had planned to commit suicide by electrocuting himself in the bathtub. I didn't realize he was in that much pain. During his life, I would give him morsels of things to feel good about, but the world around him made it hard for him to reflect on these. I was his biggest fan and advocate. We had long heart to heart talks, and he had a sense of humor that would result in side-splitting laugh attacks.

Early adulthood would add even more challenges for him to navigate through. I could guide him but had to let go of his hand. Misuse of his prescription drugs and alcohol would begin to numb his pain. I would continue to monitor him and keep positive communication going to help cut through the darkness he was feeling.

He started seeing a woman that I tried to warn him against. She was involved in drugs and newly divorced. In a couple of months, she announced that she was pregnant with my son's child. They were soon married because my son knew it was the right thing to do. They had two children, first a girl then eleven months later a boy. The relationship was rocky from the beginning, but things seemed to deteriorate once they were out on their own. He lived at home for twenty-four years, I was nervous but knew I had to let him grow on his own and learn.

He started telling me that she would physically abuse him and the children, degrade him on a daily basis and was unfaithful to him. She knew he had chronic lung disease and would continually smoke and have him and the children enveloped in a cloud of smoke. I tried to get a case manager in place to make home visits, to check up on things to help keep watch on the situation, but the process was too slow.

It was close to Christmas when the children were a couple of years old when a guy with a truck full of scrap metal told my son if he would take it to the scrap yard he would split the money with him. My son was gullible and on a fixed income, so extra money for presents for the kids sounded good to him at the time. When he arrived at the scrap yard, he was met by the police. My son explained who had given him the scrap and what he had said, but he was arrested for being in possession of stolen property. When the police questioned the other guy, he denied ever having anything to do with it and then delivered death threats to my son if he would say anything about it. My son was scared so he kept his mouth shut, did the time and paid the fine.

Dealing with a child who is mentally and emotionally challenged is pretty tough but more manageable when you have resources and support. When your child grows to become an adult, it is not that easy. Since they are adults, they feel they can make decisions on their own, and this can lead them to problems.

Addiction – condition of craving for a particular substance, thing or activity. Physiological or psychological dependence.

Center for Disease Control (CDC) from 2000 – 2014 nearly a half million Americans died from drug overdoses. **If you need help or know someone who needs help call SAMHSA National Hotline 1-800-662-HELP (4357) TDD 1-800-487-4889 (see Resources for information).**

Meanwhile, my son continued to suffer at home. Changes in meds did little to calm the confusion in his head, so he started to drink. He told me he didn't want to hear or feel anything at all. Since he was already on various medications adding alcohol was dangerous for him and caused his behavior to be very unpredictable. I suggested finding him another place to live, but he didn't want to leave the children. I tried to help and guide him as much as I could so that he could learn to make the right decisions on his own.

He had hurt his shoulder and developed a problem to where it wouldn't stay in the socket. Pain medication was added to his regime.

One weekend someone he knew came to his house and said he had a terrible toothache and requested a couple of his painkillers. So my son gave him a couple and the guy gave him a couple of dollars in return.

My son was arrested for this and charged with a felony drug sale as the guy was wired with sound and video. The attorney told me after viewing the video that he understood that my son was set up but if it went to trial that the bottom line would be drugs were exchanged for money. Now he had two serious charges on his record with a lot of unanswered questions.

He went before the judge and was ordered to attend a rehabilitation program for drugs. He was proud that he completed this program successfully. When he finished his rehab, he was still on probation and had to continue classes and be on support. When he came out of rehab, he was proud of himself and was ready for a life of sobriety.

In the meantime, his personal life was falling in around him it wasn't long before he returned to drinking again. He was drinking so much that I was seeking help through various organizations. He seemed to be out of control and couldn't help himself. They told me he had to hurt himself or get arrested before anyone could do anything; I wanted neither of those options for him. I was frustrated, I feel this is a weak area in our system when dealing with an adult who has chronic health and medical issues.

He missed one of his classes and was arrested because of his probation requirement. He spent a few days in jail which was a relief as I knew he would sober up. The judge ordered him to another rehab. My son was happy about this because he could see his own behavior getting out of his control and wanted help. This place was very different than the previous rehab he went to; it didn't have locked doors and strict confinement. He told me about various drug uses going on in the house and on one occasion, his roommate shot up heroin right in front of him. I believe he was traumatized by this experience as he told me the story over and over again and expressed how it really bothered him. He was brave enough to tell supervisors about what had happened, and the roommate was moved. He got another roommate that told him about something new that was legal; it was called synthetic marijuana. My son knew better than to smoke, because of his lungs but peer pressure was difficult for him, so he decided to give it a try.

I got a call with my son screaming in a panic on the phone because someone at the rehab house had caught him and the other guy smoking the synthetic marijuana. He was crying and hysterical, so I had to help him calm down so I could understand what he was trying to tell me. He kept saying it was legal. Unlike the other facility, at this place, you could come and go so he was walking down the street and wanted me to come pick him up. He told me that they called his probation officer, and he was scared. I told him to call his probation officer and explain what happened. He cried and said he was afraid that he would be arrested again. I explained he couldn't run or hide he had to make a call and explain. He called and was arrested.

The sadness still fills my heart. I couldn't make his decisions, and I couldn't protect him. This facility wasn't suitable for him; he needed the locked doors and structure.

About this time things were really getting worse for the children; there was drug abuse and neglect. I believe the probation officer was the one who called Children's Services as he would visit the home occasionally. I had the children regularly and never saw marks on them but at one point their mother stopped letting me come into the house, and visits with the children started getting less frequent. The day came when I got a call from Children's Services telling me they were going to remove the children from the home. The plan was for me to pick them up from school and since I regularly took them to and from school, it was an easy transition for them. My husband and I were given temporary custody. We were already raising our teenage granddaughter and now blessed with 2 more. We were later given permanent custody after their mother failed to work her eighteen-month program. The stories that would follow would grip my heart and bring me to my knees in grief for what these children had endured during their short lives. It turns out that there was a lot of physical and mental abuse. My six-year-old granddaughter didn't think she would ever be happy again. Her little spirit had been broken. My five-year-old grandson constantly cried that both of his knees hurt, he said it was where mommy would hit him in the back of the legs with the board. After clearing it medically with the doctor, it was clear he was experiencing the trauma over and over in his mind. They had experienced so much loss already in their short little lives. Now in our care, they would begin to heal.

If you suspect child abuse or neglect Call Child-Help USA Hotline 1-800-4-A-Child 1-800-422-4453

(See Resources for information)

Don't hesitate make the call!

It was time to go to court again to support my son from the smoking incident. I always got nervous in court, and I hated to see him get in trouble. This time, it was different because he was coming from jail. My heart sank as he entered the courtroom in an orange jumpsuit and was full of chains that were clanging as he walked in our eyes connected. He stood respectfully before the judge and tried to explain his circumstances. My son wasn't good with words but tried his best. The judge looked seriously at him as he told him he had been disrespectful; he didn't follow the orders as he had been before him several times. The judge sentenced him to four months in the penitentiary. I was almost in a panic in my seat, penitentiary? My mind was racing. My son is like a child in his mind, and his health is bad. I was overwhelmed with just the thought of prison. I wanted to jump up and explain, beg for mercy, something but at the same time, I didn't want to make things worse for him. The courts rules forbid you to speak to each other or even make hand gestures. We just stared at each other from our seats; I could tell he was scared. I had already learned that the judicial system didn't care about my role as his mother when he was in their care.

The process of moving from a county jail to the processing jail and finally to prison took about six months. My son wasn't a criminal he was an addict.

I think about my son's family and how their stress affected everyone. It's an incredibly lonely place. The only people who understand are those going through these experiences. My son was leaning on alcohol, his medication, street drugs, his stress was on the rise, and so were his addictions to calm it. His wife was also an addict, and the children were in chaos and being abused. It affected their entire family and ours too. If you have ever had this experience in your life, you know how helpless you feel watching the torment of the cycle. It's unbearable to watch your child suffer like this. Addiction is a battlefield going on in the mind with the voices getting louder and louder demanding their attention with euphoria being the end result.

The chains in people's lives can take many forms- addictions to drugs, alcohol, work, pornography, gambling, food, shopping, video games and even chaos. People are shackled mentally, and it can cost their lives and also affect the lives around them. The grip of bondage can be devastating, but you can find freedom from captivity.

I was exhausted and needed rest.

CHAPTER SEVEN
WINGS

Wings – can be seen as a symbol of God's presence and as an expression of one's faith.

Angels are believed to be messengers from heaven, symbolic of a guardian angel. Divine presence in your life.

Psalm 91:4 He will cover you with his feathers. He will shelter you with his wings. His faithful promises are your armor and protection.

My physically and mentally challenged son spent about six months incarcerated. This experience drained me emotionally but at the same time gave him time to get sober and reevaluate his life. He got to the point that he couldn't help himself. I had no resources at all to help him or redirect him. I prayed that he wouldn't get hurt in there. He was on medication and at one point the jail stopped the prescription. He had to wait a long time to see a doctor and get started on medication again. In the meantime, he suffered withdrawal symptoms. His anxiety was bad, and he started to cry a lot, which caused him to repeatedly pick a place on his chin until he had a bleeding sore. They put him into solitary isolation for a few days which bothered me because I knew he would be scared with no one to talk to. It wasn't his fault that his emotions were like that, he was handicapped and needed his medication. It broke my heart that he was alone, and there wasn't anything I could do to help him. I made sure he had some money so he could call home. We would write back and forth frequently.

Whether handicapped or not, your child is still your child. I sent him a calendar I made for each month with something good written in for each day. He could mark the days off so he could see the days were passing and getting closer to the time when he would be coming home.

Soon after he got home, he was divorced, and the children were still in our care. We found a one-bedroom apartment which he said felt like a palace. He continued his therapy and support; he was focused and grateful for his freedom. He met a woman about a year later. They dated almost a year and then got married. Three months later they announced they were expecting a little girl. They were excited, and we were happy for them.

Six months later I got a call from my daughter. She was in a panic and screamed: "Mom, he's dead." She had got a call from his wife who had found him slumped over and unresponsive in the living room.

When I got the call from my daughter with her screaming that her brother was dead, my mind froze. I will hear this play over and over in my mind as long as I live. It was like I was afraid or didn't want to hear what she just said. I was unusually calm, a feeling I couldn't explain.

"Who said he is dead?" I asked.

"Were his vitals checked to make that conclusion?" I questioned.

She was just going by a call she got from my daughter-in-law who first found my son unconscious. She had called 911 and was waiting for the EMTs to arrive.

I worked in the medical field for twenty-five years and thirty-three years with a child whose health was fragile. I was familiar with health concerns and even death. I had been exposed to emergency situations that required a calm frame of mind. I had always pictured his death being a gradual one in which I would be able to help.

I was stunned and in disbelief. I asked her if the emergency medical technicians had checked his vitals and if they were with him. She said she was on her way over there to check on him. I was flooded with thoughts and emotions. As she got to the apartment she told me the ambulance and first responders were there, I stayed on the phone with her. I could hear the chaos as she went inside the apartment. She started crying loudly; she was out of control. I asked to speak to the technician who got on the phone. I told him I was his mother and asked if he was deceased and the gentleman on the other end of the phone said "Yes, ma'am he is--.

My heart sank, I could barely speak." I asked quietly what would happen next, and he told me the coroner would come to get him, and they would be in contact with me in a couple of days. I was dazed by all that had just happened; I was speechless and yet I wanted to scream. The feeling of panic and desperation got the better of me. Please don't let it be true...there had to be some mistake...the feeling so overwhelming...such a flood of emotions...it's excruciating. A rush of anger would come over me, and I hit the wall with my hand as I lost my strength and collapsed.

My husband drove as I sobbed uncontrollably during the 30-minute drive to his apartment. The children were in tears, but they didn't fully understand it all. When we got to the apartment, I was disappointed that they had already picked him up. I had hoped that I would have been able to see him by myself and touch him. Somehow, it felt comforting to be in the living room where it had happened. I thought maybe his spirit was still lingering there waiting for me to come before it left.

My daughter was mad because they wouldn't let her see her brother. It's their rules and procedures when people die unexpectedly at home; they were just following protocol. His wife was visibly shaken and explained that she had laid down for a nap and found him when she woke up. She said when the technician moved him he had a can of computer duster in his lap. He was found on his knees slumped over the couch with his face buried in the middle where the cushions met in his own vomit. As I stared at the wet spot, I said quietly, "I never knew him to do inhalants." My daughter said she thought he had tried it once many years ago. Some people said it gave them the creeps to be in the room where he died but for me it's where I wanted to be. When the coroner's report came back it indicated that cardiac toxicity from computer duster was the cause of his death, it was ruled as an accident. The time of his death was said to be at 11:00 am and he was pronounced dead at 3:00 pm. It bothered me that he had laid there for four hours alone before anyone had found him.

The days to follow were very difficult, so hard to even put into words. My son had trouble taking care of his own money, so I had been his payee since the day he was born. I paid his bills as usual when another problem emerged. The bank closed his account which kept checks bouncing. He had very little money, but they still denied access to his account. I was numb during the entire funeral and burial arrangements. When my son was in his early twenties, he was on portable oxygen. He had just come off it, and the doctor had put him on a better medication to help him breathe. It just worked out that I was able to get a small life insurance policy on him because at that point he didn't have COPD or emphysema yet. I never thought I would ever use it, but it helped a lot.

In our casual conversation, we had talked about his wishes and my wishes and that neither of us wanted to go first. I was so sensitive during this time, making sure to give him what he wanted. I didn't want an autopsy, and he didn't want his blood removed. He wanted it simple. At times, I would almost panic as I was bombarded with so many emotions.

The realization that he was gone...just like that... was agonizing, gut wrenching and painful!

I kept every letter that my son sent to me when he was in jail and rehab. He had written the following letter about a month before he was released from prison.

"Hey, Mom! Well it's about 1 o'clock in the morning and I decided to write. I got your letter earlier today. Well, I got good news I have an interview for a job. It's called speak-out it is new. I'll be sharing my story with high school kids. Going out and going to high schools. It's not official but I got my foot in the door so we'll see. O I liked the pictures of the kids. I can't wait to see them and give them hugs and kisses and spend time with them. I'm going to need your help helping me to get a place to live and stuff you know. U know I know God wants me to share my story to help people. Got to get over being nervous, though. And I want you to be a part of it too. I'm still got to figure out what I'm going to say. It's funny how God works to put things in your path to do his will. I just hope and pray that God will put the words together. Somedays I feel like I was not up to par for him in the day you know. I've been checking myself as best I can to

watch what I say and do because if I act like the world then my light ain't going to shine. And it's hard at times espcilly in here. But I think I do alright. I just want to thank you MoM again for being there through my stuff and making you worry. But this is the result of my choices. So all I can do now is live everyday as best I can for him. Well I think I'm going to go to bed now. Love, Your Son, Love you Dad XOXO P.S. Tell kids I love them P.S.S. Write back I like mail.

This is written exactly how he wrote it to me.

My son and I were hand-in-hand for 33 years. After we had the private family viewing at the funeral home, my husband and I stayed awhile longer. I made a hand mold of my son. It's just a piece of plaster, but it's my son's hand. It's got his fingerprints and other details. I formed his hand into a grip just perfect for holding and now and then I would pick it up and hold it. I know it sounds silly, but somehow, it gives me comfort. I will miss our long talks, helping him manage his money, and watching over him. I will especially miss the way he could make me laugh so hard; I thought my sides would split. He was simple-minded and full of love. He wanted me to be part of his story, and he had always been a part of mine.

As I looked up into the crimson sky, the sun was low and beautiful. I felt the warm breeze brush over my face. I could hear the clicking of the pinwheels placed by the children as they were spinning around the freshly planted flowers. The cross on top of the church overlooking the cemetery gave me a comforting reminder of my faith. The picture was one I never expected to see but was somehow prepared for. The tears ran freely from a place so deep within my heart. Thoughts of his childhood, the good times, the bad times all running together. I was standing so close yet so far away, fighting to hold on and fighting to let go. I wished just for a one more moment with him. The final resting place is just that... final.

His new daughter was born two months after his death. This brought happiness to our family. He was happy she was coming. He went to every doctor appointment and picked out her name. She was due on my birthday which was special to me. She was born by scheduled C-section a couple of weeks early. It was both happy and sad at the same time to see her for the first time. It was like I could see him looking back at me through her eyes. She is our 11th grandchild and such a blessing to our family. He would have been so proud of her!

I picked up his wedding album. He was three months away from his first wedding anniversary. It was a small wedding. I was glad I took the pictures, what a treasure they are. Flipping through the pages, the tears were making it hard for me to see. He was wearing the white shirt, ivory satin vest and a tie he would be buried in, nine months later. I experienced a contrast of emotions in the midst of grieving his death.

The loss of a child is unlike any other painful loss you will ever experience. Unless you have had to walk through it yourself, you can't even imagine the pain. Emotional pain with numerous reminders, associations and triggers of things he said, things he did or places he went. The smallest things can revive the pain.

National Inhalant Prevention Coalition 1-423-902-9266

More than a million people used inhalants to get high just last year.

Children are quickly discovering that common household products are inexpensive to obtain, easy to hide and the easiest way to get high. Parents don't know that inhalants are cheap, legal and accessible products. They are as popular among Middle Schools students as marijuana. Even fewer know the deadly effects the poisons in these products have on the brain and body when they are inhaled or "huffed." Sudden sniffing death syndrome is like playing Russian roulette. The user can die the 1st, 10th, 100th time a product is misused as an inhalant.

(See Resources for information)

Speaking of wings -

I was in the medical field for 20+ years. I worked in many areas of patient care, full-time hospitals, and home care with all types of patients. I was also a phlebotomist. Yes, I was one of those people who liked to suck your blood. *grin* I am proud to say that I was one of the few people who had a painless needle and could get your blood on the first try.

Ten years ago I decided to put down the needle and switch to a camera. Remember when I said I took dancing lessons as a child and my dad arranged shows. Well, he was also a photographer. He made a darkroom in our house, and he would take his own pictures, and I was his helper. I was familiar with the process, but the one thing that always stuck out in my mind was the memories. I started an adventure of creating memories. In the mail, I got a letter that expressed the need for a bereavement photographer. I knew right from that moment it was what I wanted to do. I have been a volunteer serving area hospitals for over 10 years now. They call me if a family has experienced an early infant loss wants photos of their precious baby taken. God gave me the gift to do this, so I give it back in the way of photograph memories of their child. The hardest part for me is walking into the grief. There are absolutely no words that can be said to comfort at a time like this; it's just raw pain. My heart is always broken for these families, I was familiar with loss, so I could understand on a certain level. When my son died, I could understand so much deeper. Every photograph, every image is a treasure, a priceless memory. I want to remember all the many families and their precious little angel babies whose memories I have created over the years. I also want to praise all the volunteers everywhere who make burial garments, blankets, music, and other memory items for these precious babies and their families. I continue to answer the call when there is a need.

I Now I Lay Me Down To Sleep (NILMDTS) Bereavement Photography – Contact 1-877-834-5667

(See Resources for information)

Healing Thoughts, Daily Food, Hope for the Day- Clara Hinton Author of the Book Silent Grief – Miscarriage-Child Loss, finding your way through the Darkness.

Email:chinton@silentgrief.com

Do you need support?

Pastor of a local church can help.

There are Support Groups for whatever you might be dealing with…

Scroll down and you will see a comprehensive list. If you are in a crisis call 1-800-273-TALK (8255)

"What we have once enjoyed we can never lose. All that we love deeply becomes a part of us."

Helen Keller

CHAPTER EIGHT
BUTTERFLIES

Transformation – the process of changing from one appearance, state or phase to another.

The cycle of a butterfly holds spiritual teachings and insight for us. From an egg, the butterfly lives its early life as a caterpillar. It then retreats within the cocoon from where it is reborn as a beautiful winged butterfly.

Stage One: The Egg – fragile and delicate – Battle of growth and development.

I was born into a sinful world, gradually and methodically, I have been transformed into the person I am today. Looking back over my life it is hard to believe the many times I cried, the pain and losses I endured.

Psalm 56:8 You keep track of all my sorrow. You have collected all my tears in your bottle. You have recorded each one in your book.

This verse gives me comfort because I know that God is with me and has been with me my whole life and even knew me before I was born. When I was young, four years old, when I was adopted. *Job 29:12 For I assisted the poor in their need and the orphans who require help.*

The impact of it didn't hit me until I was bullied and shamed about it. Working through it was painful. I felt like I was unwanted, one who couldn't be loved. I found comfort after Jesus adopted me and I accepted Him as my Lord and Savior in the movie theater. It taught me that I was chosen to be loved.

Ephesians 1:5 God decided in advance to adopt us into His own family by bringing us to himself through Jesus Christ. This is what he wanted to do, and it gave him great pleasure.

I had four siblings whom I didn't know. I was the oldest. I spent very little time with them when I was in my teens. Today, I know them, and we often meet, but the distance that broke our relationships is still apparent.

I had suffered some abuse as a baby but after I was adopted I was shielded and protected from further abuse, I didn't experience it or see it in my home.

When I was in my early twenties, I would suffer physical and mental abuse from my husband. I was in the early stages of my faith. I had two little boys who were sixteen months apart. I was so afraid I would have a miscarriage due to the regular beatings I suffered during my pregnancies. There was no anger or violence in the first two years that we dated. I felt hurt, frightened and lonely. I never knew what I did to deserve the beatings. Today, when I look back, I realize that it was a lack of maturity, responsibility, and self-control on both parties; him for abusing me and me for accepting it. I remember, when my first child was seven months old, I looked up into the heavens and prayed that God would intervene. I thought he would end up killing me.

Psalm 22:24 For he has not ignored or belittled the suffering of the needy. He has not turned his back on them but has listened to their cries for help.

Sometimes you don't think God cares, or He isn't listening, but He is. After the suffering, I was able to speak out and change for the better. I started taking care of myself.

Stage Two: The Caterpillar – slow in moves, always eating, molting, shedding layers.

When my second son was a month old, my husband broke his neck in an automobile accident. He was paralyzed from the neck down. After two years of abuse, I wondered if this was an answer to my prayer. I was still concerned and compassionate and didn't want him to suffer. I stayed by his side as much as I could until he was taken to a rehabilitation center. I had my boys close by my side, our bond and dependence on each other grew tremendously over the next year and a half. I would say they were my life. Then all of a sudden, I was faced with an assault and abduction. My babies were ripped right out of my arms. I lost time and money with an attorney, and when my dad died, I lost the case as I didn't have money to continue. This time of my life is difficult to explain; it was so painful. I lost my husband, my children, and my dad too.

How do you heal a broken heart? How do you stop the ache? This knocked me off my feet. I didn't know if I would ever get back up and some days didn't know if I even wanted to. I would reach out to things to try to ease my pain. Briefly, I tried drugs and alcohol, but it just made me sick. My faith would take a growth spurt during this time. I learned that God had to be first in my life. Gently, He would remind me of certain scriptures. This renewed my growth in faith.

I had always said in prayers that my children were my life, they were my everything, but God has to be my everything first!

Luke 14:26 "If you want to be my disciple, you must hate everyone else by comparison – your father and mother, wife and children, brother and sisters – Yes, even your own life. Otherwise, you cannot be my disciple."

When my dad died, I knew I was going to have to find peace with the situation with the boys. Lack of money made my fight weaker. I always thought of my ex-husband and how he was confined to a wheelchair, paralyzed and how his life had changed. Did the boys give him something to get up for each day? Did they give him a reason to smile? I thought more of the situation of my ex-husband more than I concentrated on my life. Could this be what sacrifices feel like? *Sacrifice: to give up (something) especially for the sake of something or someone else.* The hope that God was always taking care of the boys gave me hope. Though heartbroken, I remained positive in my thoughts. I sought for peace.

Stage Three: *The Cocoon, Pupa, and Chrysalis – struggling phase*

A little while later my choice to step out of God's will and do things my way would cause a sequence of events that will forever remain in my heart. I thought someone loved me, and I ended up pregnant. He then rejected me. I always looked up to my dad and valued his decisions. He decided an abortion was the best thing for me to do. I struggled with my own guilt because I didn't stand up for my baby. I had permitted the procedure to happen. It took some time to work through my anger with my dad, but I later learned how to forgive him and myself.

Sadly, abortion cases are on the rise today! Personally, I feel like my baby and all the rest have been violated. Every baby has a right to live, but because there are people who think otherwise, a law has been put in place to silence the scream of the unborn. I didn't stand up for my baby, which was a life lost.

Jeremiah 1:5 "I knew you before I formed you in your mother's womb. Before you were born I set you apart and appointed you as my prophet to the nations."

Abortion taught me to stand up, speak out. It taught me that I am pro-life. I learned to humble myself before the Lord and to forgive myself and others. I have the assurance that I have been forgiven for my role in the death of my baby, but the hole in my heart remains.

Thank You Lord! I give you praise for the personal peace that comes from your mercy, as you release me from the torment of my sin. I will meet my baby, Precious Joy, in heaven someday.

I have been able to know the exact difference between losing a child who is alive in the womb and losing a child to death.

The anguish is equal. When my children were abducted, every day was a reminder that they were alive and every single day felt like another loss. I felt my heart breaking a little more each day.

The death of my unborn baby and my son was final; there was nothing I could do to change the situation. My living children were growing; I was missing seeing them grow up. I lived in eager anticipation hoping that tomorrow would be better but each day was a grief of its own.

I have had the opportunity to get to know my boys as adults. I bought a house down in the south where they lived and spent a few years. Even though the relationship was broken, I thank the Lord for the blessing of this season of time He gave me.

Psalm 37:4 Take delight in the Lord, and He will give you your heart's desires.

My oldest son can't accept what happened, so the distance remains which is another loss in itself. Sharing my story has helped me break out of the shell of pain and grief. I love my boys that will never change. At times I still hear their screams and still grieve the loss; I doubt if this will ever come to an end for me. At the same time, I have been able to laugh with them, cry with them and tell them that I love them. God just kept drawing me closer to Him.

I lost both of my biological and adoption parents. At times, I feel like an orphan again.

I only had my dad for 22 years and my mom for 12 more years. She lost her fight with Non-Hodgkin's Lymphoma. After my dad died, she would come and spend six months out of the year with me; this continued until she was unable to travel anymore. My parents raised me and were always there for me. They held my childhood memories and who I was. I will forever remember them and feel their love. Even in their death, they remain part of me and who I am. When they died, I had no family to cling on. God has given me a family of my own and with the love and memories of my parents, there is hope for the next generation to come.

I also lost my little sister after a 20-month fight with lung cancer about 10 years ago.

Matthew 5:4 God blesses those who mourn, for they will be comforted.

When my handicapped son was born, my walk in faith was getting stronger. I had difficulties during pregnancy and prayed that God would let my baby live. God answered this prayer. My son had special needs and was imperfect before the eyes of the world but to me, he was perfect. My faith was growing to a point I started realizing God was in control. I knew my son's life was fragile right from the beginning. I knew an asthma attack, lung infections, complications from COPD or emphysema could take his life at any time. I put him in God's hands. I had multiple spiritual lessons.

As my son stepped into adulthood, he started losing self-control. When an adult child (special needs or not) is out of control, this affects those around them. I started to experience sleepless nights, feeling helpless, and getting worried. Doubt, anger, frustration, and fear set in leading to more problems. I watched him struggle so much with impulse control complications, but I couldn't help.

What would you do with all these feeling that hit you all at the same time? I learned through experience that alcohol and drugs (legal or illegal) could not solve my problems. So I kept going, praying and seeking God. My faith was growing, and this gave me hope.

Matthew 14:24-31   Meanwhile, the disciples were in trouble far away from land, for a strong wind had risen, and they were fighting heavy waves. About three o'clock in the morning Jesus came toward them, walking on the water. When the disciples saw him walking on the water, they were terrified. In their fear, they cried out, "It's a ghost!"

But Jesus spoke to them at once. "Don't be afraid," he said. "Take courage. I am here!" Then Peter called to him, "Lord, if it's really you, tell me to come to you, walking on the water."

"Yes, come," Jesus said.

So Peter went over to the other side of the boat and walked on the water towards Jesus. But when he saw the strong wind and the waves, he was terrified and began to sink. "Save me, Lord!"

he shouted. Jesus immediately reached out and grabbed him. "You have so little faith, "Jesus said. "Why did you doubt me?"

When my son went to jail, I learned more. I had to remind myself of the story of Peter and keep my eyes on Jesus, believe and not doubt that God's word is true, and He would watch over him just like he watches over me. I would panic at times thinking he would be harmed with no one to protect him. Gently, God would remind me that He was with him, and He was in control.

Psalm 56:3 But when I am afraid, I put my trust in you.

The problems of my son and his wife together with the children got worse. The children were taken away and put in custody The extent of the abuse the children suffered was unimaginable. Their story would bring me to my knees, bruised bodies and broken spirits. So now I was watching the effect of the loss and abuse in their lives. Today, the therapy continues, the effects still real, the wounds still apparent in their lives. They join us in grief as they mourn the death of their dad.

His death was confirmed, and the grief cycle began. Unbearable grief would follow.

There are 5-stages of grief:

1. Denial – deny the reality of the situation, hide from the facts.
2. Anger
3. Bargaining – If only we did this or that.
4. Depression – Sadness
5. Acceptance – I'm at peace.

Grieving is the natural process of healing.

What is Grief – Deep mental anguish, intense sorrow, distress, to suffer from misfortune.

Depression is one of the stages of grief which is the loss of happiness.

As I walked through my son's death, between bargaining and depression, I wrestled with what if, why didn't I questions. It is so unsettling because you can't wind back time even for an instant. It's gone. It's gone.

You might struggle with this as well. My son and I talked on the phone at least once a day, but when he died, we had not spoken to each other for a couple of days. Why didn't I call him? I questioned myself constantly. I couldn't tell him that I loved him or even say goodbye just one last time. It was so sudden with no warning at all. I didn't want it to be true, but it is. The reality hits me often, and it makes me cry out 'Abba Father'! I visit his grave and weep as I try to imagine living here without him here. I know the Lord listens and understands but the hole remains.

Hebrews 10:22 Let us go right into the presence of God with sincere hearts fully trusting him. For our guilty consciences have been sprinkled with Christ's blood to make us clean, and our bodies have been washed with pure water.

I allow the feelings, gather support, and yield to the grieving process.

Stage Four: *The Butterfly- emerging from the cocoon; transformation.*

So just like the transformation of a butterfly, my life has been a series of events that has molded, shaped and prepared me for the next event. Watching people in my life encounter losses, affected my life profoundly.

My sister, who is two years younger,(remember we were separated when I was adopted?) was caught in a house fire about 20 years ago. She was severely burnt on her face and arms that she almost lost her life. Her burns required numerous surgeries. She was rehabilitated later. I watched her lose her self-esteem. She felt she was disfigured. She also lost her job as a nurse and suffered from Post-Traumatic Stress. This touched my life so much as it touched hers.

Relationships can be a temporary loss, in the case of the separation of my daughter and I or a permanent loss, in the case of divorce or death. I have had both. I didn't always understand why but I knew I had to love anyway regardless of what was happening. It's a difficult process especially when the words and actions hurt. Our first instinct is to protect ourselves and try to hurt those who hurt us or hurt ourselves.

Romans 12:14 Bless those who persecute you. Don't curse them; pray that God will bless them.

I had to practice love by exercising it as per God's Word.

I am happy to say my daughter has had two more adorable little girls, she has completely turned around. God has restored her. His word is true!

Proverbs 22:6 Direct your children onto the right path, and when they are older, they will not leave it.

I have had to work through my shame, trust issues and loss of self-worth after being abandoned in my life. Would it be a mistake if I expressed my feelings? Will I be accepted or rejected? Some people, especially in relationships, may expect you to behave in a given way and may quit if you fall short of their expectations.

Numbers 23:19 God is not a man, so he does not lie. He is not human. So he does not change his mind. Has he ever spoken and failed to act? Has he ever promised and not carried it through?

This is one of my favorite scriptures that I have hidden in my heart and have been able to hang onto.

Losing possessions and pets

There was a time when our house caught fire, and we lost everything. I had no insurance, so nothing was replaced. I was a single parent at the time. As I stood there and watched the house and everything inside burn down to ashes, I felt thankful because nobody was hurt. Our kitty, sadly, was overcome by smoke. I didn't know who to call or what we would do. We were lucky when a pastor accepted us into his home where we stayed and got back on our feet. I was humbled by the love and compassion we received as well as how the Lord blessed and provided for our needs.

I am an animal lover. A few years ago I lost my precious kitty. She was part of my family for over 18 years. She was an indoor cat, pure white with yellow/green eyes. I rescued her from a local shelter when she was 6 weeks old. You might think – she was only a cat. Yes, only a cat but a special family member who was loved. She would communicate and play in funny ways. She would play hide & seek, let me know when to get up with meows and licks, like a little alarm clock. She would meow right on time to let me know it was time for bed. She traveled with me as I lived down south and then moved back to the north again. It was heartbreaking to watch her grow old and finally, the day came that she would slip away. I grieved for days and tears still fill my eyes as I reminisce. A paw print, her ashes, pictures and so many memories of her gentle, loving nature will always be tucked in my heart and cherished! Knowing her, loving her and losing her taught me the value of a cat's life. Our love for her left a hole as well.

Let's talk about forgiveness….

Forgiveness: to give up resentment of, to grant relief from, to cease to feel resentment against, pardon.

I wanted to talk about forgiveness a little bit. As you can see, I have had people in my life that hurt me physically and emotionally. They also hurt those I loved and still love. It's very easy to harbor pain, anger and resentment. I don't believe you can truly forgive someone without God's help. In my human power, it is easy to find excuses for holding anger or grudges. It took me 24 years to forgive grandad for his assault against me when he took my babies. One day while living down south near the boys I was sitting on the lake shore asking God to help me forgive grandad. God told me to just do it. God then walked me through a thoughtful process. It was a past incident, and I couldn't change it. He reminded me of the lessons that He was able to teach me through the experience. He also made me aware of the fact that I really didn't know where grandad was in his spiritual life, and that I needed to keep him in my prayers. At that moment, by my own will, I forgave grandad for abusing me and abducting my children. I didn't go to Grandad and his wife to let them know that I had forgiven them. Grandad was having heart issues at this moment, and I told his wife I was ready to help if she needed me to sit with him at any time. This doesn't mean that I can forget the incidence, it means I let go the grudge. I don't hate them anymore. It feels good to be right with God. I had to do the same with the others who had hurt me or hurt those close to me.

Mark 11:25 But when you are praying, first forgive anyone you are holding a grudge against so that your Father in heaven will forgive your sins too.

Jesus is telling us that God will not forgive us of our sins unless we forgive others when they sin against us. So in other words, our prayers for forgiveness can be denied if we are holding grudges against others. An unforgiving spirit can hinder our prayers to God. I don't know your opinion, but I for sure don't want my prayers hindered.

Psalm 66:18 If I had not confessed the sin in my heart, the Lord would not have listened.

The Lord collects my tears, helped me, adopted me, listened to my cries, taught me to put Him first, He knew me before I was born, He didn't punish me as I deserved, He taught me to trust and not doubt, cleanses my guilt, He taught me to bless those who hurt me, taught me about training my children, and He taught me to forgive –forgive-forgive. God had a purpose for my life, and it's His perfect timing of the seasons or 'stages' in my life. He intervened. I began my journey with childlike faith. I would then go through the necessary steps to transform me into the beautiful butterfly that I am today, a new creation.

Finding rest is just one step away…

CHAPTER NINE
ONE STEP AWAY

REST –relax, refresh oneself, recover, strength, relief, freedom from worries, troubles, mental or spiritual calm.

By sharing my stories, I hope to give you some comfort. Know that you are not alone! If you have encountered a loss in the past or of recent, I said it before, and I will say it again – it hurts!

I struggled so much trying to cope with pain and other emotions that are associated with the loss. I drank alcohol alongside other drugs, had a problem with food (not enough or too much), the worst relationships and even attempted suicide but luckily it was unsuccessful.

I was able to make a spiritual connection with Jesus at an early age. A spiritual seed had been planted in me.

It is my prayer that the same spiritual seed is planted in you if you don't have one growing in you. Do you know how big a mustard seed is? Well, that is all that is needed, come just as you are!

Luke 17:5-6 the apostles said to the Lord, "Show us how to increase our faith." The Lord answered, "If you had faith even as small as a mustard seed, you could say to this mulberry tree, 'May you be uprooted and thrown into the sea; and it would obey you."

Whether you have a heart like mine, riddled with holes, I want to help you learn how to calm the ache and find rest like I have learned to. Grieving is important but from time to time you should be able to lay it aside and physically rest. Did you know there is also a spiritual rest?

Matthew 11:28-30 Then Jesus said, "Come to me, all of you who are weary and carry heavy burdens, and I will give you rest. Take my yoke upon you. Let me teach you because I am humble and gentle at heart, and you will find rest for your souls. For my yoke is easy to bear, and the burden I give you is light".

Jesus has provided His rest through our faith.

You were created by a loving God.

You have great value.

God loves you and wants to have a spiritual relationship with you.

Your sin can keep you from having a personal relationship with God and from entering His rest.

What is sin and who has sinned?

Romans 3:23 for everyone has sinned; we all fall short of God's glorious standard. Even when we aren't aware of it, we commit sin by doing the things we do (or fail to do) or by the way we think.

What's so bad about sin?

Matthew 2:23 You are so proud of the law, but you dishonor God by breaking it.

In Chapter 6, I wrote about chains and mentioned that there are many things in life that keep us bound such as addictions of all kinds. Did you know that there is a spiritual bondage? There are three links in the chain of spiritual bondage. These are – ignorance (lack of knowledge), strongholds (control over you) and deception (something that deceives you).

Sin brings us into bondage.

Isaiah 61:1 the Spirit of the Sovereign Lord is upon me, for the Lord has anointed me to bring good news to the poor. He has sent me to comfort the brokenhearted and to proclaim that captives will be released, and prisoners will be freed.

Only through Jesus can you have a personal relationship with God.

Why Jesus?

John 14:6 Jesus told him, "I am the way, the truth, and the life. No one can come to the Father except through me."

Why did Jesus have to die?

1 Peter 3:18 Jesus suffered for our sins once and for all time. He never sinned, but he died for sinners to bring you safely home to God. He suffered a physical death, but he was raised to life in the spirit.

You must personally respond by trusting Jesus as Savior and Lord of your life.

You respond with belief in Jesus.

Romans 10:9-10 if you confess with your mouth that Jesus is Lord and believe in your heart that God raised Him from the dead, you will be saved.

It doesn't mean that you have to be perfect and that you won't have any questions or that you will understand everything.

You respond by receiving Jesus.

John 1:12 But to all who believed Him and accepted Him. He gave them the right to become children of God.

One Step Away

Are you ready to take that step now?

Say this prayer and mean it from your heart…

"Dear Heavenly Father, have mercy on me, a sinner. I believe in you and that your

Word is true. I believe that Jesus (Yeshua) is your Son and that He died on the cross so that I may now have forgiveness for my sins and eternal life. I know that without you in my heart, my life is meaningless.

I believe in my heart that you, Father, raised Jesus from the dead. Please forgive me for every sin I have ever committed or done in my heart. Forgive me and come into my heart as my personal Lord and Savior today.

I give you my life and ask you to take full control from this moment on.

I pray this in the name of Jesus." Amen.

That's it!

You are now my brother or sister in Jesus (Yeshua)

You can be assured of your salvation.

John 14:20-21 when I have risen to life again, you will know that I am in my Father, and you are in me, and I am in you. Those who accept my commandments and obey them are the ones who love me. And because they love me, my Father will love them. And I will love them and reveal myself to each of them.

Your sins are forgiven.

Colossians 2:13-14 you were dead because of your sins and because of your sinful nature you were not yet cut away. Then God made you alive with Christ, for he forgave our sins.

You have eternal life.

1 John 5:13 I have written this to you who believe in the name of the Son of God so that you may know you have eternal life.

You have made the most important decision of your life. You are adopted just like me.

Salvation is a new beginning, a journey to God.

Ephesians 2:8 God saved you by His grace when you believed. And you can't take credit for this; it is a gift from God.

Begin to read your bible a little each day, start with 1 John, the Gospel of John, Psalm, and Proverbs.

Pray – simply just talk to God, He is listening.

Get involved in a local church, it helps to strengthen you and helps you grow.

Put a smile on your face and let others know, share your new found love and freedom in Jesus by what you say and do.

John 8:36 so if the Son sets you free, you truly free.

If you are already a child of God, then I invite you to join me in prayer and celebration for all who might be reading this book and take the step of salvation!

Also, remember it was unbelief that kept the people of Israel from entering the Promised Land.

Entering God's rest depends on our faith. Trust that God's promises are true. Allow your faith to bring you to a confident, secure, committed life with God. Cease from your own efforts at trying to cover your worry and your pain.

Hebrew 4:7 Today, when you hear His voice don't harden your hearts.

I took this step in my late teens, but as you can see I still struggled, I still had pain and grief from the losses in my life. He never said we wouldn't face heartache and trouble, but He promised to be with us when it touched our lives.

Psalm 34:18 The Lord is close to the brokenhearted; he rescues those whose spirits are crushed.

My heart has been overwhelmed with loss and maybe yours has been too. God has used my losses to teach me lessons that I could have only learned from Him. He has been my guide, my support, my comfort, and hope – He has been my rock to hang on to. God cares, He is powerful, and He is faithful!

1 Samuel 2:2 No one is holy like the Lord! There is no one besides you; there is no Rock like our God.

As you walk through the valley of loss, trust in the Lord!

Psalm 37:5 Commit everything you do to the Lord. Trust Him, and He will help you.

As I look over my life God's presence has been with me, he has never left me alone, he has adopted me as his own, I am his daughter, and He is my Father. He knows my name. He has used each hole left by the loss as a passage to work through, filling each hole up with his guidance, comfort, strength, healing, and love. To lead me into His rest!

Now you can receive it too! God's promise of physical rest

Exodus 33:14 The Lord replied, "I will personally go with you Moses and I will give you rest – everything will be fine for you."

God's promise of spiritual rest

Matthew 11:28-30 Then Jesus said, "Come to me, all of you who are weary and carry heavy burdens, and I will give you rest. Take my yoke upon you. Let me teach you because I am humble and gentle at heart, and you will find rest for your soul. For my yoke is easy to bear, and the burden I give you is light."

This is His promise to you too!

How do you enter into this rest?

Do you need a Bible? Call 1-855-524-2537

(See Resources for information)

CONCLUSION

We encounter losses in many forms and they will touch most of our lives in one way or another.

It hurts, but we have hope.

It hurts, but we have help.

It hurts, but we can find rest in the process.

Personally, losses have been a constant reminder of how it can be unrelenting.

What will you do if loss touches your life?

How will you cope?

How will you heal?

Psalm 46:1 God is our refuge and strength, a very present help in trouble.

Recently, I was given a gift to a mountain top retreat. While I was there, God led me to the story of Elijah. I could identify with him, one day he was up and then down the next. No matter how bitter my trials are or how hopeless my situation is, I would always know that I could depend on God's divine will for my life. Elijah was bold and other times fearful, he demonstrated defeat and victory. God had work for me to do, even when I was fearful and thought I could fail.

Prayer should be our first response to any crisis. God spoke in whispers, so Elijah had to listen to His still, small voice. The times I hear His voice is when I quiet my mind and listen.

God has been a solid rock for me to hang on during my journey that was full of life losses. I experienced emotional and physical pain which affected every cell in the body. This is the reason I used unhealthy ways to cope with my situation. I still felt lonely, depressed and desperate. Pain medications don't help they just mask over and over the deeply emotional and unresolved feelings that I walked through. God led me to that solid foundation to which I could learn to balance my emotions and see my situation positively.

God moves, teaches, loves and comforts in the midst of rain on the mountain top. Elijah went to the mountain top to pray! This gave me new energy, a new vision and a sense of purpose. Mountain top experiences are pauses that help us to refresh ourselves. When we come down from the mountain, we can face the demands of life in a better way.

Yes, I still remember my losses.

Yes, it still hurts.

Yes, I still cry.

I found the rest that only comes from a relationship with Jesus. Jesus is the source of true rest. Remember His promises? It's available to you too. You just need to believe in Him.

Hebrews 4:9-10 So there is a special rest still waiting for the people of God. For all who have entered God's rest have been relieved from their labors, just as God did after creating the world.

How do you enter into God's rest?

Remember, in chapter seven I talked about how I fight to hang on and I fight to let go? Part of entering into God's rest is to lift your hands up to Him and let go. It was a real struggle for me because I wanted to hang on tight to everyone I have lost with all my strength. Just think about how heavy that is! One loss is a heavy burden just think of multiple losses. When I let go I am still hanging on but God is carrying the heavy part, and I keep the parts that fill my heart with precious memories.

You enter when you surrender and believe that Jesus is all you need. Pray and ask Him to show you the way and He will.

Matthew 7:7 Keep on asking, and you will receive what you ask for. Keep on seeking, and you will find. Keep on knocking, and the door will be opened to you.

I know how painfully hard it is to live with loss, and it's always in the background of everything I do, but I know that Jesus loves me, and He loves you too. He understands and His open arms are waiting for me and you to surrender and enter into the rest that only He can provide.

I would like to take this opportunity to thank you for spending your time with me and allowing me to share my story with you. This tired and weary path is a lonely journey but with Jesus lighting the way to hope and rest He leads us to victory.

I would like to pray that you receive this blessing from Numbers 6:24-26

Pray along with me and receive it -

May the Lord bless you and protect you.

May the Lord smile on you and be gracious to you.

May the Lord show you his favor and give you his peace.

Amen

Resources

Chapter 1
Child Welfare Information Gateway (08-2013) Penny Border & Portnoy 2007, Impact of Adoption on adopted persons. Washington D.C., US Department of Health and Human Services – www.childwelfare.gov

Chapter 2
2015 Safe Horizon   2 Lafayette Street, 3rd floor New York, NY 10007 1-800-621-HOPE(4673)
2015 Stop violence Against Women

Chapter 3
Why Family Take Children, Vanished children's Alliance, the National Center for Missing and Exploited
Children (NCMEC) www.childabductions.org 1-800-843-5678 or Find The children 1-888-477-6721
California Child Abduction Task Force.

Chapter 4
Prolife America, Prolife.com Project 1840 South Elena Avenue, Suite 103 Redondo Beach, CA 90277
424-247-7490 HOTLINE 1-800-712-4357 Councelors 24/7 jtfinn@earthlink.net

National Suicide Prevention Lifeline 1-800-273-8255 anytime 24/7 English and Spanish
Deaf or TTY 1-800-799-4889 Immediate Medical Crisis Call 911

Chapter 6

Child-HelpUSA 24/7 Child Abuse Hotline 1-800-4-A-Child 1-800-422-4453

4350 E. Camelback Road, Bldg. F250 Phoenix, AZ 85018

Substance Abuse and Mental Health Services Administration (SAMHSA)

National Hotline 1-800-662-HELP (4357)

TDD 1-800-487-4889 – 5600 Fishers Lane Rockville, MD 20857

Chapter 7

Now I Lay Me Down To Sleep (NILMDTS) Bereavement Photography – Their mission is to introduce

Remembrance Photography to parents suffering the loss of a baby with a free gift of professional portraiture. To find a photographer 1-877-834-5667

www.nowilaymedowntosleep.org/find-photographer/

Silent Grief.com P.O. Box 92 Shanksville, PA 15560 Email: chinton@silentgrief.com

National Inhalant Prevention Coalition 318 Lindsay Street Chattanooga, TN 37403

423-265-4662 or 423-902-9266 www.inhalants.org

Mental Health America 500 Montgomery Street, Suite 820 Alexandria, VA 22314

Phone 703-684-7722 Toll Free 1-800-969-6642

Crisis Line 1-800-273-TALK(8255)

www.mentalhealthamerica.net/find-support-groups

Chapter 9

United States Bible Society 1-855-524-2537 5544 Forest Drive
Loganville, GA 30052
info@bibles4free.com

Support

www.griefshare.org
www.SilentGriefsupport.com
www.mentalhealthamerica.net/find-support-groups

Author Bio

Teresa Collins is a non-fiction writer from Ohio. She is an active volunteer bereavement photographer for families who experience early infant loss. She is retired from the medical field with 25 years experience.

At an early age, she has suffered an infant loss, which was then followed by several other losses. Life may have been tough for her, but she won't allow anything to bring her down. For that reason, she finally decided to share the reflections of her heart and personal insights through writing.

Although she knows challenges and problems can be thrown her way, she still sees the brighter side of life. In fact, she wants other people to be inspired by hope and encouragement from her story. Along with her husband, grandchildren and their 180lb. Mastiff, Teresa will continue her journey to heal, to cope and to grow in the Lord.

I love this company and wanted to share with you....

I have some classic bands I enjoy and recently received a couple custom bands in memory of my son.

MudLOVE

Handmade pottery and jewelry

- In the fall of 2009, wheels were turning (potter's wheel that is). Inside of a tiny garage, big dreams were becoming a reality. With nothing more than an old stamp set, a box of clay, and a plan to support clean water projects in Africa handmade creations emerged, and MudLOVE was born.

- Get hope. Give hope is a collaboration with a local nonprofit, the Humanity & Hope United Foundation. Over the last 5 years, H & H has built relationships with villages in Honduras, helping those trapped in the cycle of poverty to learn, grow and prosper. Every 'Hope' band you purchase will create 1 day of employment for someone in a Honduran community.

- MudLOVE offers bracelets in classic, cursive, animal and custom bands. I ordered a custom band that says 'Angel Wings' with my son's name and year of his death. The purchase of a custom band will provide one week of clean drinking water to someone in need. They also make Pottery – Classic Mugs and Big Mugs.

Please visit www.mudlove.com and read their full story, check out their products help them spread encouragement and inspiration.

They are also on
Facebook, Instagram, Pinterest and Twitter.

Made in the USA
Middletown, DE
01 July 2016